Thoughtings

Thoughtings

Puzzles, Problems and Paradoxes
in Poetry to Think With

Peter Worley and Andrew Day

 Independent Thinking Press

First published by

Independent Thinking Press
Crown Buildings, Bancyfelin, Carmarthen, Wales, SA33 5ND, UK
www.independentthinkingpress.com

Independent Thinking Press is an imprint of
Crown House Publishing Ltd.

© Peter Worley and Andrew Day 2012
Illustrations © Tamar Levi 2012

British Library Cataloguing-in-Publication Data
A catalogue entry for this book is available
from the British Library.

Print ISBN 978-178135087-4
Mobi ISBN 978-178135091-1
ePub ISBN 978-178135092-8

Printed and bound in the UK by
TJ International, Padstow, Cornwall

For Katie, Leo, Lawrence, Oliver, Alexander,
Rose, Aldo, Sara, Jimmy, Emily and Max.

May you continue thoughting.

Contents

Contents

Foreword, or Forward? Or Backward? Or in both directions at the same time?
by Michael Rosen

This collection of poems is very, very irritating. It's irritating like having toast crumbs in your bed. It's irritating like having toast crumbs in your brain. Let me explain: most of the time we go about looking and listening, talking and playing, making things, going places without wondering too much too often why exactly we're doing it. It's as if it's all one great big flow of stuff: get up, have a wee, wash, breakfast, out the house, school or work, do stuff, come home, watch TV, have something to eat, argue with some people you live with, go to bed. Or something like that.

All the time this is going on very nearly all of us are using words and phrases. But what are they for? How do they work? Do they just tell us what's there, what we have to do, what we should do? Or are they a bit more mysterious than that? Are they secretly attached to strange ways of thinking that we only know about when someone points it out. Do you remember a scene in Alice in Wonderland where there is an argument about whether 'I mean what I say' is the same as 'I say what I mean'? The more I think about that, the more it feels like toast crumbs in my brain.

Well, this book is like that. It's full of puzzles and possibilities. It asks us questions but they're not the kind of questions that necessarily have a right or wrong answer. They might be the kind of question which might have several right answers, or even no answer at all. It might be a question which is just a puzzle that we can sit and think about as a puzzle, something amazing or odd about the way we humans think and speak.

No matter how old or young we are, we're all used to the idea that school and education is about stuff that we have to get to know. It's in books, on the internet, on worksheets and on the whiteboard. Every day, we're supposed to get hold of some of that stuff, get more knowledge or more skills. Meanwhile, that secret thing I spoke about is going on. We're not only learning stuff. We're also learning how to think ABOUT stuff. We get set in our ways of thinking. We might get to think, say, that if it's written down in a book, it must be right. But what if it isn't? How could you tell? What kind of thinking would you have to do, to figure out that what was written on the page is wrong? And if it is wrong, how did it get put in the book? Was someone just wrong or were they trying to trick you? How could you tell?

More toast crumbs in your head?

Well, I did warn you. But maybe you didn't believe me. Or maybe I'm wrong.

Anyway, this is a book of thoughtings. Thoughtful, thought-making pieces of writing.

One last thing: getting toast crumbs out of your bed is fun. They jump up and down. Some of them refuse to be swept out. Some of them find new places to hide. Some invite you to nibble them. Getting toast crumbs out of your mind is just like that too.

A Thoughtroduction
by Peter Worley and Andrew Day

Everything in our collection of *Thoughtings* was inspired by the thoughts of children as voiced to us in our daily work, visiting primary school children and running philosophy sessions. We turned their insights, brainwaves and verbal entanglements into puzzles and poems for the young – and when we took them back to the classroom, they went down a storm.

Once teachers saw how engaging these pieces were for their pupils, they started to ask us how to get hold of them. So we've collected them together and expanded their range. They can be read for fun or used as a starting point for discussions. Many of them also get children thinking about language itself.

Children love pondering big, philosophical questions like, 'Does the universe end?', 'Where is my mind?' and 'Can something be true and false at the same time?' These verses capture that impulse in the growing mind, and feed it further.

If you want to know how we use these poems with children turn to Appendix I on page 191. Regularly updated lesson plans that make use of these *Thoughtings* are available if you become a member of The Philosophy Foundation website (www.philosophy-foundation.org). You can find a sample lesson plan in Appendix II on page 195.

Here's to the joy of puzzlement!

Question to class:

What is thinking? But try to answer without
saying the word 'thinking' in your answer.

Year 1 (age 5) child:

It's when you're thoughting.

Introduction

Are Things Always What They Seem To Us To Be?

Are things what they seem to us to be?
'The sky is blue,'
Or so say you
But I am not so sure.

The sky *looks* blue
But when it's night
It isn't any more.

I have a chair and it is green
And my friends agree
That it is green
When they've seen
My chair.

But turn off the lights
And the green is gone
Yet can you say to where?

Are things always what they seem to us to be?
Please read on and take the time to think on it for
me …

Questions for 'Are Things Are Not Always What They Seem To Us To Be?':

❖ What is *colour*?

❖ Is the colour of a chair *in* the chair itself?

❖ Where is the colour of something?

❖ If you put a green chair in a *completely* darkened room what colour is it?

❖ If two people disagree about what colour something is, who is right? How would you know who is right?

❖ Is how something looks the same as how it is?

❖ Is 'looks' the same as 'is'?

❖ Are things always as they seem to us to be?

Minds and Brains

The Thought

I had a thought
I kept it in my mind
Where's that?
My mind is in my brain
Which is in my head
Which is under my hat.

Questions for 'The Thought':

- ❖   What is a thought?
- ❖   Where is a thought?
- ❖   What do you need to have a thought?
- ❖   Can you say what a 'thought' is without saying the word thought in your answer?
- ❖   Can you control your thoughts? How?
- ❖   Can you share your thoughts? How?
- ❖   Can you get or know someone else's thoughts? How?

The Thought Fight

A thought fight broke out in my head.
'I'm right', 'No, I'm right!' both thoughts said.
Thought One was the one I first believed,
And it started to cheer, thinking success achieved.

But then Thought Two spoke up, loud and clear,
Starting to win round my inner ear,
When again Thought One took up its case,
And argued its way back into first place.

Thought Two was not a quitter though
And it too had a second go
And proved itself mentally resourceful,
With reasons that were sound and forceful.

They fought as hard as sister and brother,
Interrupting, contradicting each other.
I would have thought both thoughts if I could
Because they both sounded equally good.

Why must I choose?
Make one win and the other lose?
They answered: 'There has to be a victory.
The two of us are contradictory.'

Questions for 'The Thought Fight':

- ❖ Do you agree that one thought has to be the winner?
- ❖ How could one be the winner? How would it win?
- ❖ Do you ever have two contradictory ideas?
- ❖ Could the two thoughts in the poem stop fighting each other?

Ideas

Ideas,
Where do they go?
Without them
What do I know?

Are they tall?
Or thin?
Or thick?
Or round?

Are they something
You need?
Do they have
Any sound?

Ideas,
Where are they from?
What can I think
When I have none?

Are they small?
Or big?
Are they real?
Or not?

And what happens
To ideas
That have been
Forgot?

Ideas,
I want to have more
And more
But can I be sure
No one's had them before?

Questions for 'Ideas':

❖   What is an idea? (Can you say what an 'idea' is
     without saying the word idea in your answer?)

❖   Where do ideas come from?

❖   Where do they go?

❖   What came first: a chair or the *idea* of a chair?

❖   What is more real, a chair or the *idea* of a chair?

❖   What do ideas do?

❖   Is there an idea of an idea?

❖   Are ideas a human invention?

❖   Are ideas invented or discovered?

❖   Are there different kinds of ideas?

Can I Think?

Can I think?
My human friends
Don't think I can

But I think:
I think I can think.

Okay, so I'm just
Nuts and bolts
And made to work
With wires and volts

But I think:
I think I can think.

But if I'm wrong
And really I can't,
I only *think* I think I can think?

Questions for 'Can I Think?':

- ❖ Can a computer think?

- ❖ What is thinking? (Can you say what 'thinking' is without saying the word thinking in your answer?)

- ❖ Do you think the robot that is thinking this poem can think? Why?

- ❖ What does 'I think: I think I can think' mean? Does it make sense?

- ❖ Do you think robots will be able to think in the future?

- ❖ What does a robot or computer need to have in order to be able to think?

- ❖ If a computer says that it 'thinks that it can think' can the computer be wrong?

Between My Ears

How much space is in my head
That my skull is made to cover?
A smile of intelligence
From one ear to the other.

There's a kind of thing that has no width
That I keep on putting into it.
My brain is only a few inches wide
My mind, however, is infinite.

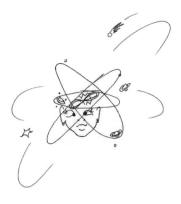

Questions for 'Between My Ears':

❖ What is between your ears?

❖ What is a 'smile of intelligence'?

❖ What is it that you can keep putting into your head that has no width?

❖ If your brain is only a few inches wide, how can your mind be infinite?

❖ Is your mind infinite?

❖ Is your mind the same thing as your brain, or are they different?

❖ What is a mind?

❖ Where is your mind?

❖ What does your mind do?

❖ What would happen if you didn't have (1) a brain or (2) a mind?

❖ If you 'change your mind' do you also 'change your brain'?

Word Wonders

A Long Word

Philosophy's a long word
Not everyone can say it
Lisophophy? Physolophy?
Silly-oso-billy-olo-soppy-if-a-loff-a-lee?
That's what it sounds like to me.

They could make it shorter
Cut off a quarter
Then it would be Philoso
Or Losophy.
Or if instead you kept the quarter
And threw away the rest
That might be best.
Then you could call it Phil
Or Phy.
Perhaps I will.
It's easier for me.

Questions for 'A Long Word':

* Philosophy comes from a Greek word. How did they say/pronounce it? (The Greek word is φιλοσοφια [pronounced: fi-lo-so-fee-ya]. If they pronounce it differently from us, is it the same word?)

* Why do we use long words?

* We sometimes make long words shorter so that they are easier to say (e.g. maths, phone, telly, DVD = digital versatile/video disk). Is it OK to do that?

* Should someone say a word in a way that is easier for them (like in the poem) or the same way as everyone else?

* Can you say *philosophy*?

* Can you say *Silly-oso-billy-olo-soppy-if-a-loff-a-lee*? Can you say it quickly?

* What do you think the word *Silly-oso-billy-olo-soppy-if-a-loff-a-lee* means? Can it mean anything?

* Philosophy means 'love of wisdom' in Greek. What do you think 'love of wisdom' means?

* Where do words come from?

* What is a word?

Nosense

Nobody knows
That I have no nose
How many more 'no's
Will it take

To prove that my nose
Knows nothing it knows?
So, 'no' no more 'no's
For Pete's sake!

Nobody's 'no's
Can prove what they know's
That the bones in your nose
I will break

If you don't stop your 'no's,
Take your thumb out your nose,
Coz everyone knows
That it's fake!

Questions for 'Nosense':

- ❖ Does this poem rhyme?
- ❖ How many different versions of the sound 'noze' can you find? Can you explain them?
- ❖ Why is it called 'Nosense' rather than 'Nonsense'?
- ❖ How many different meanings can you find in the title?
- ❖ What is a *homophone*? Are there any in this poem?
- ❖ Does the poem make any sense?

Punktuation

The teacher sighs:
'What is a sentence?'
The child recites:
'A sentence is this:

It always begins
With a capital letter
And ends
With a little full stop.'

The teacher says:
'Nice one,
Now get up
And write one!'

The child gets up.
Then, taking his pen,
Writes at the top
Of the board:

S. *[The reader should write this up on a board rather than say it out loud.]*

Questions for 'Punktuation':

- ❖ Do you think the boy is being naughty or not?

- ❖ What is a sentence?

- ❖ Do you think he should be punished?

- ❖ What does the title tell you, if anything, about this poem?

It Started in the Library

Over the door of the library
You can see the word 'library'
So that you know it's the library.

When you get to the door
There's nothing on the door
To tell you it's a door.

But what if there were?

What if you made sticky labels
And stuck them to the doors, chairs and tables?
And a label on every book
Saying 'book'
So you could identify it with one look.

And then you kept going
Beyond the library
To every wall and car and tree
To rocks and sand
And then the sea!

Could be hard.

It would be even harder to label birds!

You'd need a never-ending supply of labels
But you'd never run out of words.

Questions for 'It Started in the Library':

- ❖ How do we know what something is if it doesn't have a label?

- ❖ Are words labels?

- ❖ What is a label?

- ❖ What is a word?

- ❖ Will we be able to find words for everything or will some things always be beyond words and labels?

- ❖ Would you ever run out of words?

The Wronger

I'm a wronger
I try to right
But I get everything all mixy
I haven't got the slightest might
Of successing
With I's guessing.

Today anothers were all writing,
Sentencing neatly in straight lines.
But my words did wanders and wonkies
People else's were bettering mines.

I wish I had a bit of clever
To help me when I'm classing.
I could confidence and brave exams
And get well done for my passing.
But it's not my happen ever.

I've tried to learn what the teacher is taughting,
But there's something wrong with my way of
thoughting.

Questions for 'The Wronger':

- ❖ Does the poem make sense?

- ❖ Can you translate the poem into better sentences?

- ❖ Are the poet's sentences wrong?

- ❖ What makes a sentence right and what makes a sentence wrong?

- ❖ Read the first stanza of Lewis Carroll's 'Jabberwocky' and say whether the stanza makes sense or not. Then say whether you think it's grammatical or not.

Metaphor

What's a metaphor?
What's a metaphor *for*?

Why is a hurricane a *hungry beast*?
Why is a painting a *visual feast*?
How can the sun *climb* in the sky?
Or clouds – which are vapour – ever *roll by*?

A metaphor's a word that stands for
A thing that it's *not*.
So is 'it' a metaphor?
Or 'what'?

Word Wonders

Questions for 'Metaphor':

- ❖   Why do we use metaphors?
- ❖   The poem asks what a metaphor is. Do you think the poem answers that question?
- ❖   The poem asks if the words 'it' and 'what' are metaphors. What do you think?
- ❖   If we have a word, does that mean there must be a thing that the word means?

A Town Called *That*

Verse 1
There once was a town called That
Two men came to it so that
They could paint a new sign
Declaring that That
Is worth a visit and friendly and that.

The first man he started his 'That'
The other, he did just that.
'It's a competition,'
Said the judge about the mission,
'So make sure that your "That" is FAT!'

When they'd finished
The judge he said
That that 'That' that that man painted
Is fatter than that 'That' that that man just did.
But no one knew which 'That'
That judge liked best
So the little town of That
Remained signless for guests.

Verse 2

There once was a town called

That-that-that-that-that-that-that

Two men came to it so that …

Verse 3

There once was a town called

That-that-that …  ¹

Two men came to it so that …

[*Can you finish verses 2 and 3? Bet you can't!*]

---

1   The sign ∞ is a mathematical symbol that means infinity. Here it means 'to infinity'.

Questions for 'A Town Called *That*':

❖   Can you read out loud all three verses correctly, making sure your 'that's are correct?

❖   There are different uses of the word 'that' in this poem. How many can you find?

❖   Why is the third verse impossible to finish?

❖   Find out what a Möbius strip is. (It is where the sign for infinity comes from!)

❖   In the second verse do you replace every occurrence of the word 'that' with 'That-that-that-that-that-that-that'?

❖   Why did no one win the competition?

Word Wonders

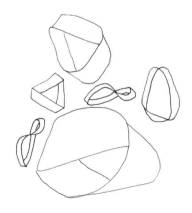

The Rhyme Behind the Rhythm

[*Note to the reader*: Read this poem to your audience twice. The first time you should leave out the last *italicised* phrase and see what your audience thinks goes at the end of each couplet. The second time, read out the poem in full. This should give you the controversy needed for this poem and any discussion around it.]

Does a good poem always have to rhyme?
If it does not then is it a …
criminal act? (Alternative end-word: 'crime')

Does it need always to be outwardly said
Or can it be silently said in your …
imagination? (Alternative: 'head')

Should it be something the poet implies?
And if she does not has the poet told …
fibs? (Alternative: 'lies')

Does a rhyme or a rhythm have to pretend
To promise to deliver a predictable …
last word? (Alternative: 'end')

But it needs to be somewhere concealed
in the lines
So that the young reader can hear that it …
has words that sound the same! (Alternative:
'rhymes')

Questions for 'The Rhyme Behind the Rhythm':

- ❖ Does this poem rhyme?

- ❖ How many poems are on this page?

- ❖ Do any of the words in the poem give you clues as to how to answer the first two questions?

- ❖ Is there a clue in the title?

- ❖ You need to decide whether you think the poem (1) rhymes, (2) doesn't rhyme or (3) rhymes *and* doesn't rhyme! (Some of the other questions may give you a clue as to how to answer this task.)

- ❖ When the poem says the word 'it', what does it mean?

You, Me and My Shelf

Can I write a poem with one less word on each line as
it moves its way down the page? Can I form a shape
with my meanings so that all I say is contained
in triangular rhymes and rhythms that hold
up the top of my page like a piece of
architecture of word and poetry-
play that fits just here for
you like a shelf for
you to
say?

Questions for 'You, Me and My Shelf':

- ❖ How do you think you should read this poem? Is there more than one way it can be read?

- ❖ Why is the poem shaped like it is?

- ❖ Could you give the poem the same shape if you recited it?

- ❖ Are there other ways you could shape a poem in a creative way?

- ❖ Try writing a 'shaped' poem of your own.

The Quest

Once there was a knight
With sword and armour and white horse.
His king said, 'I have a quest, will you do it?'
The knight said, 'Of course.'

'I want you to go
To the top of the Jagged Mountain,' said the
King,
'And kill the dagger-toothed dragon that breathes
fire and gas!'
The knight said, 'Your Majesty –
just one thing …

I cannot do as you ask
So I might be condemned for treason
For though I have horse, sword, armour and
brave heart,
I do not have … a reason.'

'A *reason*?' cried the startled King.
'What a strange thing for you to mention!
I've never heard of such a thing.
I must see this new invention.'

'So, young knight,' he said,
'Ride out on your horse with this new
command:
Search the world till you find a Reason
And bring it back to our land!'

Questions for 'The Quest':

❖ Do you think kings should have to give reasons? Why?

❖ Should we do what people tell us if we are not given a reason? Always? Sometimes? What does it depend on?

❖ Is it possible for the knight to find a Reason and bring it back to the kingdom? How?

❖ Is there a reason for everything?

❖ Do we ever do things for no reason?

❖ Do we have to have a reason to do something?

Without an 'M' in the Alphabet ...

I wouldn't be able to enjoy my food
Nor make a sound when lost for words;
Without an 'm' cows can't *moo*
Nor *move* backwards, sideways or forwards.
And when we fall out I can't *mend*
What is broken, it's just an *end*.

Questions for 'Without an 'M' in the Alphabet …':

❖ Do you agree with the poem? Are the things the poem claims true?

❖ Can you think of a sound that we use that has no letter to represent it?

❖ Can you invent a new letter?

❖ Can you find sounds in other languages for which there is no equivalent in English?

❖ Do you think there are any letters missing from our alphabet: abcdefghijklmnopqrstuvwxyz? If so, where would the missing letters have gone?

The Sesquepedalianist

Young Bigwordius Borus
Read the English thesaurus.

He said 'It's one of my idiosyncrasies
To employ obscure terminologies.'

A little while ago
He fell in love with Jo.

For over a week
He was too shy to speak,

Then thought, 'I'll write my inamorata a letter
Why vocalise when the written word is better?'

'Devoutly worshipped Jo,' his note began
And for ten pages of long words it ran.

It ended, 'I prophesy a splendid future for us.
I'm perspicacious, you're pulchritudinous.'

Jo wrote back, the very same day
In a very different way:
'Dear Bigwordius,
No.
Yours,
Jo.'

Questions for 'Sesquepedalianist':

- ❖ What kind of words does Bigwordius use? Why?
- ❖ What's the difference between Bigwordius and Jo?
- ❖ Why do you think Jo says 'No' to Bigwordius?
- ❖ What do you think a Sesquepdalianist is? What about the other words in the poem? How can you find out?
- ❖ Do we need long words in our language? Could we just say everything we want to say with shorter words?

Poems To Do

How Long Is a String of Letters?
(Shakeable version)

… woenaisasrtinigorfleaterswtnotinetgtoelthelm
aprtexcetmneuaningcholpasedavlltodgeithertehe
ndremingdinlgthestortthhtwahethpneeyseouthw
itheacfhholthpaerthenHwasneerndobtbuntnotw
thtteyregoingorevernitestotpetdtoaskhowlogisast
rigofletrs …

Shake the book and turn the page
To see what the letters have fallen to make
Shake it up and turn the leaf
To see if there's meaning underneath …

How Long Is a String of Letters? (Shaken version)

… Howlongisastringofletterswithnothingtotellth
emapartexceptmeaningcollapsedalltogetherthee
ndremindingthestartthatwhentheysetoutwitheac
hothertheendwasneverindoubtbutnowthattheyr
egoingforeverneitherofthemstoppedtoaskhowlo
ngisastringofletters …

Questions for 'How Long Is a String of Letters?':

❖ How long is this poem?

❖ Where does this poem begin?

❖ Where does this poem end?

❖ The letters on the previous page are the same letters as on this page but in a different order. Is it the same poem? Is the other one a poem at all?

❖ Do we really need spaces between words?

❖ Where does meaning come from?

❖ What is meaning?

❖ What is the meaning of meaning?

Order!

There once a writer was
Who had a idea clever.
He sat to write a down poem
To the thought record forever.

But one the words of he chose
Had independent an mind.
Along it ran the sentence
To sit its friend behind.

Noticing this, other soon words
To shift decided about,
Moved to and where they wanted
To chat to their and mates chill out.

Author threw down the his pen
Up and picked the troublesome page.
'I order order you to get in,'
He eyes bellowed, his blazing with rage.

The little words just giggled but
Refused to and rearrange,
Leaving the sentences author's
Terribly looking strange.

Though you, the reader, be able might
To read them in the order right …

Questions for 'Order!':

❖ What's different or strange about this poem?

❖ Can you understand it anyway?

❖ Does it matter which order we put the words in a sentence?

❖ Why is the poem called 'Order!'?

❖ Can you put the poem's words into a better order?

❖ If you order the words better is the poem better?

Is There Something In It?

Inside I mhigt be all jelbmud up
Eevn thguoh on the oustide
I look, to all apaearpnces,
Fnie, dadny and brgiht-eeyd.

Tehy say taht lokos are depecitve:
'Dno't jdgue a book by its ceovr!'
But do you tihnk you shluod let tihs
Rlue yuor lfie foerver?

Trehe is seomtnhig in it, *obscured*
Smtehiong, but I cna't qutie tlel
Wehhter it's a porepr wrod
Or a wrod taht jsut cna't slpel!

Questions for 'Is There Something In It?':

- ❖ How is this poem understandable?
- ❖ Does a word have to be spelt correctly?
- ❖ Does a word have a correct spelling?
- ❖ Why is the word 'obscured' not obscured?
- ❖ Should you judge a book by its cover?
- ❖ Where is meaning in a word? On the inside, the outside or somewhere else?

Invisible Punctuation

We shouldn't say bad things about our friends.

 We shouldn't say bad things about our friends.

We *shouldn't* say bad things about our friends.

We shouldn't *say* bad things about our friends.

We shouldn't say *bad things* about our friends.

We shouldn't say bad things *about* our friends.

We shouldn't say bad things about *our* friends.

We shouldn't say bad things about our *friends*.

How many meanings are we left with in the end
If we say, 'We shouldn't say bad things about our
friends',
Over and over again?[1]

---

1 Based on an idea from *Introduction to Logic* by Copi and Cohen (Prentice Hall, 2008).

Questions for 'Invisible Punctuation':

- ❖ How many meanings can you find in this poem?
- ❖ What is invisible punctuation?
- ❖ Can meaning change just with tone of voice?
- ❖ Do words catch meaning exactly?
- ❖ If you say a word over and over again does it lose its meaning? Why?

Death by Punctuation!

[*Hint*: Take in a BIG, DEEP breath before you begin.]

> There's one thing that you must remember to do
> though it's sometimes not easy to let the air
> through when you're given a poem with no
> punctuation or commas or full stops or slight
> fluctuation of tempo and pacing and it just won't
> stop racing and saying it's getting much harder to
> do but make sure that you breathe in a circular
> loop coz *a poem like this is tempting to try but you*
> *really must breathe SO AS NOT TO DIE!*

If you thought that was easy then try this one:

Death by Puncture!

[*Hint*: Take an even deeper breath for this one!]

> There's one thing that you must remember to do
> though it's sometimes not easy to let the air
> through as you feel yourself getting more and
> more tired and you can't stop yourself going
> down like a tyre when you're given a poem with
> no punctuation or commas or full stops or slight
> fluctuation of tempo and pacing and it just won't
> stop racing and saying it's getting much harder to
> do but make sure that you breathe in a circular
> loop coz *a poem like this is tempting to try but you*
> *really must breathe SO AS NOT TO DIE!*

Questions for 'Death by Punctuation!':

- ❖ Why do we need punctuation? *Do* we need punctuation?
- ❖ What does punctuation do?
- ❖ Does punctuation affect meaning?
- ❖ How would you punctuate 'Death by Punctuation!' and 'Death by Puncture!'?
- ❖ Is it easier to read with punctuation?
- ❖ We can't see any punctuation when we speak, so why do we need it for writing?

Archaeology

How many poems have *not* been written?
How many have never found their way
Out of the people who would have writ them
If they'd managed somehow to find their say?

I'd like to make a beautiful anthology
Of all the poems that never were
But it's going to take a special archaeology
To dig up what only *might* have occurred.

So why don't you start my sizeless collection,
Because in this happy book they'll be no rejections,
And write a lucky poem that would never have been
If it weren't for the poem that you've just seen?

Questions for 'Archaeology':

- ❖ Do things that only *might have happened* happen somewhere?

- ❖ If you do something like eating cereal instead of toast is there a world where you ate toast instead of cereal?

- ❖ What do you think someone who died young might have done if they had lived? Is there a possible world where they did live?

- ❖ Has this poem allowed something to exist that wasn't going to exist? If so, has this poem created only what might have happened?

Anthology of Unwritten Poems

Write yours here …

Or visit www.anthologyofunwrittenpoems.com to discover more unwritten poems.

Number Wonders

Infinity Add One

'How many is infinity?'
That's what I asked my dad.
'A lot,' he said, and shook his head
So maybe I said something bad.

'Is infinity a lot?' I asked,
The next time I saw my best friend.
She's one year older, but shrugged her shoulder
And our discussion came to an end.

'Infinity is the highest number,
you keep adding noughts forever,'
Was my teacher's reply, I don't know why,
But teachers are meant to be clever.

'So what's infinity add one?'
That was my very next question.
'I don't know, so why don't you go
And google it?' was her suggestion.

'Infinity add one,' I typed,
And searched the whole internet.
I scrolled through pages and pages
But haven't understood any yet.

So where can I find the answer?
Is there even an answer to find?
Or none at all, after all
To be found by the human mind?

Questions for 'Infinity Add One':

- ❖ Do you think there is an answer to the question 'How much is infinity add one?'

- ❖ What is infinity?

- ❖ Can you have infinity minus one? If so, what number would you be left with?

- ❖ Is infinity possible?

- ❖ Is it possible to think of infinity?

- ❖ Find out what a Möbius strip is.

6,800,000,000

Six billion eight hundred million
Is the number of people on earth.
Another way to say it is six thousand eight
hundred million,
Or six point eight billion, too.
Is it true?

The number goes up when a baby is born.
Down when someone dies, and people mourn.
But is the actual number right now,
The same as the people we've got?

All I can say is that another way to say,
Six billion eight hundred million is …
A lot.

Questions for '6,800,000,000':

- ❖ [*Before reading the poem!*] How do you say the number in the title? Is there more than one way to say it?

- ❖ Do we know how many people there are in the world? How?

- ❖ Does the number go up or down, or both? Why? How do you know?

- ❖ Can the number ever be right? How?

The 2-Square

2   2

2   2

Look to the *twos* that make up the square
How many *numbers* do you think there are there?

[*Note to reader*: Stop here and allow a discussion
before reading the next part.]

And is there a square *any-which-where*
To be found at all when you stand and stare?

[*Note to reader*: Allow for another discussion after
the second verse.]

Questions for 'The 2-Square':

- ❖ How many numbers are there in the 2-square?

- ❖ How many different answers can be found to the question above?

- ❖ Which answer is right?

- ❖ If someone says there are no numbers, what reason might they have for saying this?

- ❖ What is a number?

- ❖ Where can numbers be found?

- ❖ Is there a difference between a number and a symbol of a number?

- ❖ Is there a square behind the twos?

Base 10

1 = nothing else
2 = me and you
3 = family
4 = fair and square
5 = the growth of trees
(See also the Fibonacci Series)
6 = snowflake shapes
7 = the time I wake
8 + hate = arachnophobic
9 = octopus with a walking stick
10 = 'The End'
… or is it *equal* to 'start again'?

Questions for 'Base 10':

- ❖ Can you explain why the phrase for each number has been chosen?

- ❖ Research the Fibonacci series and see if you can find out what it has to do with the number 5. And what have trees got to do with both?

- ❖ Research snowflakes to see what they have to do with the number 6.

- ❖ Can you answer the question at the end of the poem?

- ❖ What can you find out about 'base 10'?

Prhyme[1]

1. Prime
2. Number
3. Poetry.
5. Thread through our numbers,
7. A secret sequence lies hid.
11. Found in old Egypt, known by the wise Euclid.
13. Numerical mysteries for you to discover:
17. Study this poem with care, and their nature you too shall uncover.

---

1 Thanks to Robert Torrington for writing 'Prhyme'.

Questions for 'Prhyme':

❖ If you study this poem, what do you uncover? (*Clue*: syllables)

❖ What can you spot that is special about prime numbers?

❖ Are there any other number sequences?

❖ Can you write your own poem which follows a 'secret sequence'?

❖ What other kinds of codes or messages can you hide behind words?

❖ Do you think there is a biggest prime?

❖ What are prime numbers?

❖ What are numbers?

Two Twos

Ug said to his brother Mog,
'Let's make a bet.
When we go out hunting today
I'll catch more deer than you get!'

Mog was feeling confident.
He said, 'I'll shake hands on that.
I'm a better hunter than you.
You couldn't catch a rat!'

All day they roamed the hills
Hunting deer to eat,
And in the afternoon
Came back to their cave to meet.

'Look at my four deer,' said Ug.
'You have only caught two.
I've won the bet, and I have proved
I'm a better hunter than you.'

Mog didn't speak, but turned around
And went out hunting for more.
He came back with two more deer
And dropped them on the floor.

'You've still lost to me!' said Ug.
'You've just caught two again.
And don't you try to trick me,
I can count all the way to ten!'

So sadly Mog agreed with Ug
That he had lost the bet.
If only he'd known, two twos are four,
But it hadn't been invented yet.

Questions for 'Two Twos':

❖ What kind of people are Ug and Mog?

❖ Who wins the bet? Why?

❖ Do you think 2 + 2 = 4 was invented by someone?
How would they have done it? Or was it always true
before anyone knew it?

Number-Land

Are numbers found
In Number-Land
Where there's nothing else but numbers of
numbers?

What do they eat
When they want a salad
Are there special kinds of cucumbers?

What do they count with
When they want to find out
How many live in the *number-hood*?

Is there a Number-Land
For numbers to use
So the number of numbers is understood?

Questions for 'Number-Land':

- ❖ Where are numbers to be found?
- ❖ Is there a special place for numbers?
- ❖ What is a number?
- ❖ If you wanted to count numbers, would you use numbers?
- ❖ Are numbers invented or discovered?
- ❖ How many numbers are there in this sentence? [*Write this up on the board.*]

Puzzles and Paradoxes

Impossibling

Today I'm going to do impossible things
And when I do, I call it 'impossibling'.
When *impossibling* you've got to take it a step at a
time
Because drawing round squares takes practice
you'll find
But if you keep on trying
If you persevere
Then logical contradictions
Are nothing to fear.

'One and one is two'
Is boring though it's true;
It's much more fun
When you make it equal to
'Seven plus four'
Which gives 'eleven'.
It's still 'one and one'
In impossible heaven.
See how easy *impossibling* is
If you add 'wrong and wrong'
It equals all this …

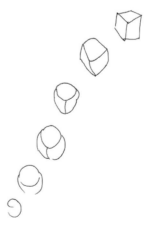

More Impossiblings ... [1]

Can you lie while standing?
      (Then tell the truth lying down.)
Can you move whilst still?
      (Are you *still* moving around?)
Can you love while hating?
      (What if hating's what you love?)

Can a top be a bottom
      (If the bottom is above?)

Is there one *and* many
      (If you have a bowl of fruit?)
Are you dressed while naked
      (When you wear your birthday suit?)

Is there nothing left to us
That it's impossible for us to do,
If we spend our days *impossibling*
And making wrong things true?

So, don't let impossibility
Get in the way of solving things,
If someone says, 'You can't do it!'
Then just try *impossibling*.

---

1 For the first read-through leave out the bracketed lines and see if your audience can think of their own impossible answers to the questions. Compare them with the poet's own answers.

Questions for 'Impossibling/More Impossiblings … ':

- ❖ 'Nothing's impossible!' Discuss.

- ❖ Is the poet really doing impossible things? Why or why not?

- ❖ Why don't you try *impossibling* for a day? Did you manage to do an impossible thing? How easy or difficult was it?

- ❖ Is it possible to do the impossible?

The Other Hand

When you go into my house
The shed is on the left-hand side.
When you come out
It's on the right.

That's easy to understand
But on the other hand …

What if there's no one at all in sight?
Is it on the left-hand side
Or the right?

Questions for 'The Other Hand':

- ❖ What do the words 'left' and 'right' actually mean? Could you explain it without pointing or showing?

- ❖ What's the difference between down and up?

- ❖ Does a cylinder have a left and right side?

- ❖ Could something have a left but no right?

This Poem Is False

If it is, it isn't,
If it isn't, it is.
That's how a paradox goes.

So, if this poem is true
Then this poem is false,
But that's crazy coz everyone knows

That if something is true
Then it can't be false
And if something is false
It can't be true.

But take another look
At this poem (*and* this book)
And you might begin to see
What seems awkward, over-long and wrong,
Seems true
Suddenly.

Questions for 'This Poem Is False':

- ❖ Is the title true or false?

- ❖ What is a paradox?

- ❖ Does a paradox prove that it is possible to do the impossible (see questions above for 'Impossibling')?

- ❖ Can you research some other famous paradoxes (e.g. the liar's paradox or Zeno's paradoxes – such as the arrow paradox or Achilles and the tortoise)?

Tralse

If I'm not here then am I there?
And if not there then am I here?
Here, there, there, here!
Is there anywhere else I can be?
Is there somewhere in between?
Somewhere squeezed in
That just can't be seen?

If it's not true then is it false?
If not false then is it true?
True, false, false, true!
Is there possibly something else
In the middle of true and false?
Could there be such a thing as
Tralse?

Questions for 'Tralse':

- ❖ Is it possible to have something that's in between true and false?

- ❖ Is it possible to have something that's in between here and there?

- ❖ What does 'true' mean?

- ❖ What does 'false' mean?

- ❖ What would 'tralse' mean if the poet got his way and it became a word?

- ❖ Can we make up words?

- ❖ Where do words come from?

- ❖ Can something be both true and false?

- ❖ Can something be neither true nor false?

- ❖ Can something be half true and half false?

A Disappearing Riddle[2]

When I'm there you can't see me.
When you kick me it won't hurt.
If you look I'm invisible.
When I talk I'm not heard.

I can be whatever you want
Though I am *I-don't-know-what*!
I'm always around you
In between every spot,

I fill every gap,
Every space,
Every crack.
What am I?

'Are you ____?' [*The reader has to try to fill this in before continuing.*]

[*The poem should be read twice: once up to the open question with discussion and then again with the last two lines followed by more discussion.*]

I'll tell you – *nothing*.
How 'bout that?

---

2 This came from a session with a Year 3 class in which a child was trying to describe the word *nothing* and the rest of the class had to guess the word. Almost all of them said, 'Is it God?'

Questions for 'A Disappearing Riddle':

- ❖ What is nothing?

- ❖ Is nothing something?

- ❖ The poem seems to have been written by nothing itself. Does that make sense?

- ❖ Is it possible to describe nothing?

- ❖ Is it possible to think of nothing?

Socrates' Puzzle

There's only one thing I know
And this thing that I know
Is something I know for certain.

Some say, 'No, no, no!
There's loads that we know
And plenty we know for certain.'

But I say, 'I know
That the *one* thing I know
Is that I know *nothing* for certain.'

Questions for 'Socrates' Puzzle':

- ❖ Why is this a puzzle?
- ❖ What does he know?
- ❖ Is this a paradox? Why or why not?
- ❖ How does he know what he says that he knows?
- ❖ How do you know what you know?
- ❖ Do you know anything?

You, Me, Aliens
and Others

From Me To You

How can I get
From here to there
When when I'm there
It's here?

And when I get there
I'm here again
And here
Has turned into there.

I wonder what
Tomorrow is like
So I lay down
And hurry to then,

But when I wake up
Tomorrow's today
And I'm back
To square one again.

How can I change
From *me* to *you*
If not from
Here to *there*?

Or is it something
I can never do,
Like trying to round
A square?

So that I may be
You and not *me*
I wonder
What I must do.

Well,
When I am me,
From your point of view,
I'm not *me* at all
I'm *you*!

Questions for 'From Me To You':

❖   This poem is confusing. Can you explain:

   1.   The first two verses?

   2.   The third and fourth verses?

   3.   The fifth, sixth, seventh and eighth verses?

❖   Where is 'here'?

❖   Where is 'there'?

❖   Does the poet succeed in becoming 'you' and not 'me'?

❖   Can you ever get to tomorrow?

❖   Can you ever be 'there' and not 'here'?

❖   Is it possible to round a square?

❖   Can you think of something that is completely impossible to do?

An Other Poem

I'm trying to be other
Than where I am
Trying to be other
Than *who* I am
Trying to be other
Than what there is
I'm trying, but brother!
I'm failing at this.

Another other I want to try
Is being behind another's eye
Where I'll look on the world
With new shades of colour
That I never would see
If I wasn't another.

Questions for 'An Other Poem':

- ❖ What would it be like to look out from someone else's eyes?
- ❖ Would it be possible to look out from someone else's eyes?
- ❖ Can you be someone else?
- ❖ Do you think everyone sees in the same way? How do you know?
- ❖ What does 'other' mean?

The Yeah-Coz-Fingee

A boy saw a yeah-coz-fingee
Standing at the bus stop.
If you see a thing like a yeah-coz-fingee
Suddenly you just stop.

'You look strange!' said the yeah-coz-fingee.
'Me?' said the boy. 'What about you?
Why have you only got one eye?' the boy asked.
The creature said, 'Why have you got two!'

'Tell me,' it said. 'Do you see two streets,
Two bus stops and two of me?'
'Of course I don't!' the boy replied
To the creature, who came up to his knee.

The yeah-coz-fingee looked carefully
'You've only got one mouth,' it shouted.
'One mouth is all I need,' said the boy.
It was something he had never doubted.

'You mean …' the yeah-coz-fingee gasped
'You eat and breathe and speak with one?
Absurd!
And what's more,' the creature sneered,
'It's the most disgusting thing I've ever heard.'

'Look at my face,' the creature continued,
'Each of my mouths has a duty.
One eats, one speaks, one breathes, you see?
And, three's the right number for beauty!'

'Well,' said the boy, defending himself,
'One mouth's totally normal for me.
Your separate mouths eat, breathe and speak
But my clever mouth does all three.'

'Another thing that makes you weird,'
Said the yeah-coz-fingee, impolitely,
'Is you've only got two legs to walk.'
The little thing was laughing slightly.

'So what?' said the boy, annoyed and hurt,
'I don't feel jealous of you.
Anything your eleven legs can manage
I can do just the same with two!'

The creature said, 'If you lift one leg
It's obvious that you'll fall down.
What kind of job could you ever do,
Except be a circus clown?'

'Watch this!' the boy called back
And took ten steps along the pavement.
'Impossible!' the creature whispered,
Its one eye wide with amazement.

'What a fascinating specimen!'
The yeah-coz-fingee said to itself.
'I'll take you to my science lab,
And keep you in a jar on the shelf!'

Questions for 'Yeah-Coz-Fingee':

❖ What is a yeah-coz-fingee? Can you draw one?

❖ What does the yeah-coz-fingee think about the boy? Why?

❖ Do you think the yeah-coz-fingee is strange? Is the boy strange?

❖ What's the difference between strange and normal?

Pencil Person

I'm a person all made of pencils
Well, maybe not quite *all*
I've pencils for arms and legs
A box for a body
And my head is a ball.

So, here's a question for you
To get you chewing *your* pencils:
How many things am I?
Am I *One* or *Many*?
Though clearly made of utensils.

[*Make the Pencil Person on the table or floor and discuss it at this point, answering the questions in the second verse.*]

You see the problem I have?
Am I pencils, a box or a ball?
I've come to this conclusion:
I wouldn't be here,
I wouldn't be asking,
If it weren't for the sum of them all.

Questions for 'Pencil Person':

* If you follow the instructions and make a pencil person, how many things are there on the floor?

* How do you decide how many things something is?

* If two people disagree about how many things Pencil Person is, who's right? How do we know who's right?

Who's That?

Who's that
In the mirror
Staring back at me?
Is it my reflection
That makes me ask this question:
'Who is she?'

Could she be
Asking that of me?
Speaking simultaneously
So I can't hear her question to me:
'Who is she?'

Questions for 'Who's That?':

- ❖ When you look in a mirror who do you see?
- ❖ Who does the person in the mirror see?
- ❖ Could you be a reflection of someone looking in another mirror on the other side of your mirror?
- ❖ Can you ever really see yourself as you are?
- ❖ Who sees you as you really are?
- ❖ Who are you?
- ❖ What's the real you?

Thing-a-Me!

You always know where it is
It cannot hide from you,
Except perhaps when you sleep –
When awake, it's good as new.

It goes wherever you go
Unseen by any eye
And no one else can have it
However hard they try.

It buzzes in a single spot
Like electricity,
And switches on just like a light
At your delivery.

I said it has a name to it
But you'll know it by its *feeling*.
Can you guess what it is?
I've always called it '_ / _ _ / _ _ _ _ _'!

Questions for 'Thing-a-Me!':

- ❖ What is the poem describing?
- ❖ What is a thing-a-me for the poet?
- ❖ Are there any clues in the poem?
- ❖ What is 'me'?
- ❖ What makes you 'me'?
- ❖ Does a robot have a 'me'?
- ❖ Does an animal have a 'me'?
- ❖ Does a rock have a 'me'?

That's Me

My name is not the same as me.
You can call me Mohammed,
Christian, Lucy or Dave.
Or you can call me Running River
Like a Native American brave.

You can call me stupid.
You can call me ugly.
Call me strange.
Laugh at my clothes, my family, my voice.
I won't change.

The most important thing is not affected.
Deep within, it's well-protected.
Unless I show you, you can't see
The heart of everything. That's me.

Questions for 'That's Me':

❖   What does the poet say is at the heart of everything?
    Do you agree?

❖   Would you still be you if you didn't have the same
    name?

❖   If someone changes their name, do they change?

❖   If we call people stupid or ugly, does it change them?
    Does it change us?

❖   Why does the author say you can't see them if they
    don't want you to?

What Fred Said

A serious man called Fred
Thought serious thoughts, and he said,
'All of the people who know they're the best
Should look after themselves and forget the rest.
The weak and ordinary are bad
To worry about them, well, that's mad.
It's not your problem if they fail
Does a lion care about a snail?
If you yourself can be great
Be great now, before it's too late.'

Questions for 'What Fred Said':

- ❖ Why does Fred talk about a lion and a snail?
- ❖ Is it your problem if other people fail?
- ❖ Do you think anything could ever change Fred's opinion?

Where's Mr Nobody?

Where's Mr Nobody?
I can't seem to find him.
And wherever I look he's
Not there.

We were talking together
About mythical creatures
That inhabit a land called
Nowhere.

I say 'talking together',
But he didn't say much
Or have a great deal to
Say to me.

But that's why I like him
Coz he always agrees
And I don't disagree with
Nobody!

Questions for 'Where's Mr Nobody?':

- ❖   Where is Mr Nobody?
- ❖   Where are mythical creatures?
- ❖   How many horns does a unicorn have?
- ❖   Can you talk to someone who's not there?
- ❖   Can something be 'not there'?

Socrates

There was a man called Socrates
He had a big belly and knobbly knees
His beard was white and fuzzy as cotton
His head was bald as a baby's bottom.

His eyes were bulgy and his ears stuck out
His nose looked like a piglet's snout
He was famous for being so ugly
But something about him was really lovely.

Crowds of people would follow him round
They all came running when they heard the
sound
Of Socrates in the street each day
They'd all press in, asking, 'What did he say?'

But there were others listening in
Who thought, 'He's evil – this is sin!
We have to stop this ugly thought.
Arrest him – take him off to court!'

What did he say that alarmed them so?
Just this: 'My friends … what do you know?'

Questions for 'Socrates':

- ❖ What was lovely about Socrates?
- ❖ If you knew Socrates, do you think you would like him or not?
- ❖ Is Socrates' question easy to answer?
- ❖ Is it possible to have a beautiful mind? If it is, is it better than a beautiful face, or not?

Space, Time and
Other Weird Things

Atoms

We can't see atoms
But we know they're there.
There's a million billion atoms
In a single strand of hair.

Everything's made of atoms,
Each table, each pencil, each chair.
Even water's made of atoms
And there's atoms in the air.

But wait … I *can* see atoms!
Whatever scientists say.
Because my hand is made of atoms
And I see it every day!

Questions for 'Atoms':

- ❖ Can we see atoms?
- ❖ Is everything made of atoms?
- ❖ Are atoms made of atoms?

Where Did Yesterday Go?

Where did my teddy go?
He's under the stairs.

Where did my blanket go?
Not into thin air!

Where did my dinner go?
Mmm, into your nappy!

Where did my tears go?
They turned into 'happy'.

Where did my birthday go?
You had it yesterday.

Where did *that* go?
Yesterday? That I cannot say!

Questions for 'Where Did Yesterday Go?':

- ❖ Where did yesterday go?
- ❖ Is the past still there? (Does the past exist?)
- ❖ Is there any way that we can get yesterday back?
- ❖ Can you explain each of the answers that are given in the poem?
- ❖ Why can't they answer the last question?
- ❖ What is the past?

A Birthday Surprise!

I can travel backwards
Or keep going straight
Sideways, left or right.

But can I go *through* time
Forwards or backwards;
Do you think that I might?

I wish I could
Coz then I would
Say 'Hello!' to my mummy.

But for a birthday surprise
I would say 'Hello!'
just *before*
I popped out from her tummy!

Questions for 'A Birthday Surprise':

❖   Would it be possible, with a time machine, to travel to a time before you were born?

❖   Would it lead to a contradiction (i.e. that it is both true and false that you have not yet been born)?

❖   Will a time machine one day be built or would a time machine be impossible?

❖   Would it be possible, with a time machine, to meet yourself?

❖   If you did meet yourself when you were younger, what might you say to your younger self?

The Law of Grab-ity

The ground is greedy
And very needy,
It always clings to me.

Try as I might
I can't shake it off, I'm
Like a fly in a jar of honey.

As I was saying:
The floor is greedy
And it snatches what I find

And when I drop
My round of toast
It licks the buttered side.

The ground is greedy
And very needy
It wants me close and when

I stand up straight,
Though from *Homo erectus*,
It trips me up again.

Questions for 'The Law of Grab-ity':

- ❖ What is being described in this poem?
- ❖ How does the speaker in the poem understand what is being described in this poem?
- ❖ How old do you think the speaker is?
- ❖ Is the ground greedy?
- ❖ Does the ground cling to us?
- ❖ What does *Homo erectus* mean?

Littlest

(For Peter's three-month old daughter Katie)

How little is little?
How big is big?
Can little be little alone?

Or does little need big
So that it can be little
And hide so it can't be known?

Is there such thing as littlest?
Can something be smaller
Than the tiniest thing
There can be?

Well, whatever the answer
I know that *my* 'Littlest'
Is littler and lovelier
Than me.

Questions for 'Littlest':

- ❖ Is there a smallest thing?
- ❖ Is there a biggest thing?
- ❖ If there was only one thing in existence, would it be big or small?
- ❖ How big is big? How little is little?
- ❖ Is bigness itself big?

Petering

My shout
It falls like a stone,
Unless there's an echo
To carry it back home.
Unless there's an echo
To carry it back home.

My past
It drops like a pebble
Leaving a trail
Of temporal rubble.
Leaving a trail
Of temporal rubble.

An echo's a bit
Like a boomerang:
The harder you try
To throw it away
The harder it comes
Around again.
The harder it comes
Around again.

That memory
Keeps repeating
Fainter each time
'Til I can't recognise
Where my echo
Began its petering.
Where my echo
Began its petering.

Questions for 'Petering':

- ❖ What is the past?
- ❖ Does the past exist?
- ❖ When did the past begin?

A Time Machine

I really could do with a time machine
I'm late for class: *it's history!*
When time is lost
Is it gone forever?
Or can we get it back
With a little endeavour?

But wait a minute
I *do* have one!
And I'm travelling in it
One second at a time.
Just think about it,
Don't look at me oddly,
My time machine is
Well, it's my … body!

Questions for 'A Time Machine':

❖ Is your body a time machine?

❖ If not, what is a time machine?

❖ Do you think it would be possible to build a time machine?

❖ What is time?

❖ Do the past and future exist?

❖ What would happen if you went back in time and met yourself?

❖ Is your future up to you or is it already planned before you get there?

❖ What does the poet mean when he/she says, 'I'm late for class: *it's history!*'? Is it a history class they are going to?

❖ What would you do with a time machine?

Space

Does space end?
And where does it start?
Is it what's in between things and keeps them
apart?

Is space anything?
Or nothing at all?
Is it space that fills an empty bin or ball?

Can space move?
Is it in one place?
Is it the hundred metres you run in a race?

Can you get rid of space?
Or cut a bit, or change it?
Maybe humans can't, but could God arrange it?

Where does space go?
Is there any spare
When you take up space and put a thing there?

Is there just one space?
Or lots of different bits?
And is each space the right shape for the gap it
fits?

Questions for 'Space':

- ❖ Can you answer any of the questions in the poem?
- ❖ Is space something or nothing?
- ❖ Can we change space?
- ❖ What happens to space when we fill it up?

Possible World?

What if things didn't turn out
The way they in fact did
And something different
Had happened to me instead?
Would I still be 'what if-ing'
In another possible world then?
Can you 'what if?' in a 'what-if?'-world
Back to what is certain?
And what if I carry on 'what if-ing'
Each and every day,
Then might I just 'what if?' too much
And 'what if?' myself away?

Questions for 'Possible World?':

- ❖ What is a possible world?

- ❖ Do possible worlds really exist?

- ❖ Could the real world be a possible world from the point of view of a possible world from the real world?

- ❖ Could things have happened differently to how they actually happened?

- ❖ Are there some things that could have happened differently and some things that couldn't have happened differently? What would they be?

- ❖ Is a 'possible world' even possible?

Mostly Made of Space

An atom is mostly made of space
And atoms make everything else.

That means that everything else
Must be mostly made of space.

Both me and you are made of atoms
And atoms are mostly made of space.

So if atoms are mostly made of space
Then mostly most of you isn't there at all.

Questions for 'Mostly Made of Space':

❖ What is the poet trying to say?

❖ Do you agree with what the poet is trying to say?

❖ If not, which bit do you not agree with?

❖ Why does the poet say that we are mostly made of space?

❖ If we are mostly made of space, does that mean that most of you isn't there?

❖ Do you need to research about atoms and then see if you agree with the poet or not?

Light from Stars[1]

Near

Far

Here

Star

A glistening memory of a distant past.

Me

Here

You

There

I look at you, you return my stare.

If

We

See

Each other

I on Earth, you another

Each of us, a different time

Spaced by distance

Never climbed.

---

1 It takes light from the sun approximately eight minutes to reach the Earth, so we only ever see the sun as it was eight minutes ago. It takes some distant galaxies 17 billion years for their light to reach us. (Remember, you should never look at the sun directly with the naked eye!)

For you to see me
I'm in *your* past
For me, you
You're in mine.

If we see each other
Then we do so strangely,
Each in two pasts
At different times.

Questions for 'Light from Stars':

❖ What does the poet mean by 'two pasts at different times'?

❖ How can they both be in each other's past?

❖ Does the fact that we see stars as they were rather than how they are mean that we travel through time when we look at stars?

The Stone

If I trip over a stone tomorrow
Was I *always* going to kick it?
If I'm going to trip on it tomorrow
Can I possibly avert it?

I could look out for stones,
Avoid them at all costs,
Take control of my bones,
Try not to get lost.

Will it work do you think?
Or is that little stone
Just sitting there,
Waiting for me
To stumble into it?

Questions for 'The Stone':

- ❖ Can you avoid what is going to happen in your future?
- ❖ What is your future like?
- ❖ Is it already there waiting for you?
- ❖ Do you make your own future?
- ❖ Does the future already exist?
- ❖ If God knows your future does that mean that it is already fixed?
- ❖ If God knows your future do we have free will?

Flow

I was watching the river running over the rocks
I looked away as I took off my shoes and my
socks
When I dipped my feet in with a gasp and a
shiver
I suddenly wondered: is this the same river?

I mean …

Sometimes it's high, sometimes it's low
It can race right past, other times it's slow
And as I waggle my feet going numb in each toe
Watch more water coming and then watch it go
A question emerges – so, I'd like to know:
Is a river a thing, or in fact just a flow?

Questions for 'Flow':

- ❖   Is there anything that doesn't change?
- ❖   Does everything flow/change?
- ❖   Can you step in the same river twice?
- ❖   What makes a river the same over time (if anything)?
- ❖   Is that true of all things or just rivers?

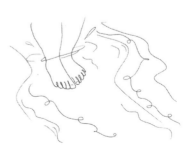

How Do
You Know That?

Colour

The snow fell in the dark.
I awoke to a wonderful sight.
Everything had changed colour
Before it got light.

Except the lines in the middle of the road
Which were already white
Right?
Am I sure?
Mmmm. Not quite.

Questions for 'Colour':

❖   Did everything change colour because of the snow?

❖   If the snow fell in the dark what colour was it?

❖   If snow falls on a wooden bench that is painted green, what colour is the bench: white, green or wood colour?

❖   If everything was the same colour could we see anything?

History

First of all was the Romans
They built the Pyramids
And bridges, roads and theatres
And cities all planned out in grids.

I know there was the Tudors
Henry VIII had seven wives
Like lots of people in those days
His wives all had short lives.

The Victorians were after that
They beat the Germans and built schools
But they were strict and serious
And punishments were cruel.

One day *we'll* be history
Something for children to learn
What name will History give us
When it is our turn?

Questions for 'History':

- ❖ Is everything in the poem true? Which bits are/aren't?

- ❖ How do we know what happened a hundred or a thousand years ago? What would happen if we got our facts wrong?

- ❖ What do you think children will learn about us when we are History?

- ❖ What name could people of the future give us (like Romans, Victorians, etc.)?

The Capital of France

Paris is the capital of France.
That's what it says in the books.
It's an easy fact to find out for anyone who looks.

Paris is the capital of France.
But how do you really know?
The books, the teachers, the internet and
everyone says so.

But how do you know they know?
You know they know because they know they
know and they tell you so.

But then, how do they know that they know?
Because other people told them so.
So …
How do they know that these other people who
told them so know?

If you keep asking how people know
You can see which way it's going to go.
You'll end up saying: how do you know that
those people who told those people who told
those people who told those people who told
those people (all that time ago)
know?

Questions for 'The Capital of France':

- ❖ Is the poem clear or confusing?
- ❖ How do we know that Paris is the capital of France?
- ❖ Is it possible that we could be wrong about it? Why or why not?
- ❖ Where do facts come from?

Love, Goodness
and Happiness

The Wicked Which

Let's play a little game
Just for the next one hour,
Let's imagine that you find a ring,
A ring with a special power.

When you put it on
It does something incredible;
When you put it on
It makes you turn invisible.

You're encircled by a choice now:
To decide just how you'll use it.
Should you pick it up?
Or should you just refuse it?

Which do you think you would do
With your new-found special power?
Which do you think you *should* do:
Good or bad?
(Just for the next one hour.)

Questions for 'The Wicked Which':

- ❖ If you found a ring of invisibility, what *would* you do with it?
- ❖ If you found a ring of invisibility, what *should* you do with it?
- ❖ What's the difference between the two preceding questions?
- ❖ If you can't get caught, then is it okay to do whatever you choose?
- ❖ If there's no chance of getting caught, is there any reason to do good?

Miss Not Unhappy

She never cried
She never frowned
Or made a discontented sound

She never griped
She never groaned
Muttered, grumbled, yelled or moaned

She never swore
She never cursed
Complained, or whined, or thought the worst

She never sighed
Or sang sad songs
Or mentioned any hurts or wrongs

She never … we'll, there are so many things
So many moments that time brings
She never did, she never saw
I ask: was she rich or poor?

Questions for 'Miss Not Unhappy':

- ❖ Do you think bad things ever happened to her?
- ❖ Would her life be better if more bad things had happened to her?
- ❖ Was anything missing from her life?
- ❖ Would you prefer a life with good things and bad things, or always in the middle?

What Is Happiness?

What is happiness?
Where can I find it?
Is it hiding behind the door?
And if not this one
Then perhaps the next
Hides that nice feeling I had before.

What is happiness?
Where can I find it?
Is there somewhere where it's stored?
And when I find
A little of it
Please, sir, can I have some more?

Questions for 'What Is Happiness?':

- ❖ What is happiness?
- ❖ If you find it then can you keep it?
- ❖ Is happiness inside you or outside you?
- ❖ Where is it?
- ❖ Is happiness a feeling or something else?
- ❖ Is happiness important? How important?

I Love My Nan

I love my nan
I love my mother
I love my brother and they love me

I love being warm on a windy night
And I love a girl in class 4B

I love my auntie
And both my uncles
And I love my Nintendo Wii

I love football
I love my boots
And shin-pads
And I love Chelsea

I love baked beans
I love toffee
I love cartoons on TV

I love snow
I love hot sun
Sports day, the end of term – *yippee!*

What a lot of things I love
What a lot of things love must be.

Questions for 'I Love My Nan':

- ❖ If you made a list of things you loved, how many things do you think would be on it?

- ❖ Are there any things in the poem that everyone loves? Are there any that no one really loves?

- ❖ Is love lots of different things? Or is it the same thing?

Am I Good?

When I play football
I'm good at that,
When I'm nasty
I'm nasty to
My annoying sister,
Some teachers at school;
Sometimes,
I'm good at being cruel.

And other times
I'm good to people,
I hold doors open,
I'm thoughtful too.
Does that make me
A good person,
Someone nice,
One of the few?

I'm left with this question:
What sort of person
Makes others both happy *and* sad?
One conclusion
I've reached for certain is:
I'm very good
At being bad.

Questions for 'Am I Good?':

- Is the poet good?
- What is good?
- Can someone be a good person and a bad person?
- Are there good people and bad people?
- Does the poet's final conclusion answer the question the poet has asked in the title?
- Is there more than one meaning of the word 'good' in this poem?

The Ship of Friends

Is it the first one I ever made?
Or the one who, when I owed money, paid?
Perhaps the one who never lied?
Or the one who always took my side?
Which of them above the rest
Is the biggest one of all, the best?

Is it who I call or text the most?
Or is it the very generous host?
The one who's rich and gives me half?
The one who always makes me laugh?
Maybe someone dead and gone?
Unless … can I have more than one?

Questions for 'The Ship of Friends':

- ❖ What is the poem about?
- ❖ How can you tell?
- ❖ Do you think any of the poet's ideas is the correct one?
- ❖ What makes a best friend?
- ❖ How many real friends can someone have?
- ❖ Why did the poet choose this title?

Naughty-Land

If one day you walked and walked
And walked and walked and walked,
Then walked and walked
And walked and walked
Then walked a little more,

Until at long, long, long last
You discovered a long lost city,
One where the inhabitants
Did things a little differently.

In this new-found civilisation
They reward the naughty children
And punish the well-behaved ones
For doing what was told to them.

Would you want to live in this place?
Do you think it's best for you
To live in Naughty-Land and do
Just what you want to do?

Questions for 'Naughty-Land':

- ❖ Would you want to live in Naughty-Land?

- ❖ What does 'naughty' mean?

- ❖ Would the people of Naughty-Land be good people or bad people?

- ❖ Is it right for the people of Naughty-Land to be naughty?

- ❖ Do the people of Naughty-Land have a right to be naughty if they want?

- ❖ If you go to Naughty-Land should you behave as they do?

- ❖ Should you teach them to be good?

Happy Sad

I hate happiness
It gets me down.
If people laugh
It makes me frown.

They say that everyone
Wants to be happy,
I disagree, to me
Happy's sappy!

When everyone's happy
It makes me feel bad
Because I'm never happier
Than when I'm sad.

Questions for 'Happy Sad':

- ❖   What is happiness?

- ❖   What is sadness?

- ❖   Can happiness in others make you sad?

- ❖   Can your own happiness make you sad?

- ❖   Do you think the person in the poem has ever experienced happiness?

- ❖   Does everyone want to be happy?

- ❖   Do the last two lines, 'I'm never happier than when I'm sad', make sense?

- ❖   Can you enjoy being miserable?

School Rules

Are Opinions Never Wrong?

Are opinions never wrong?
My teacher says they're not.
She says we're all entitled
To express our opinions a lot.

But what if I say, 'A square is round'?
Am I entitled to that?
Coz if I am, then I'm entitled
To pass my stupid SATs

With whatever I want
To put in the box
Where the answer's meant to be.
I'm entitled to be as wrong as I like
And still pass gloriously.

So who's to say what's wrong and right
In tests and examinations?
Surely I'm *entitled*
To answer with falsifications!

Questions for 'Are Opinions Never Wrong?':

- ❖ Are opinions never wrong?

- ❖ Is everyone entitled to their opinion?

- ❖ If someone is entitled to their opinion, does that mean that their opinion can never be wrong?

- ❖ Can your opinion be wrong about this: 'I love the taste of Marmite'?

- ❖ Can your opinion be wrong about this: 'I think that $1 + 1 = 2$'?

- ❖ Can your opinion be wrong about this: 'I think that $1 + 1 = 3$'?

- ❖ What is an opinion?

Do It

If you say do it, I don't
If everyone joins in, I won't
If the sign says stop, I just go
If it says speed up, I go slow.

Left is my right, no is my yes
I won't eat my dinner or breakfast unless
I make up my mind to do it myself
(So put those Corn Flakes back on the shelf!).

No one can change me or make me obey
Rules or instructions in any way
I'm in charge here, I control everything
In the world where I live that makes me king.

Questions for 'Do It':

- ❖ Is it possible to always decide what you do yourself?
- ❖ Is it possible to decide nothing yourself?
- ❖ Would life be better if you only did what you decided?
- ❖ Do you want anyone else to make you do things? (If you do, are they really making you do it, or are you really deciding?)

Big School

When I go up to the big school
I have a clever plan.
I'm going to bully other kids
As much as I can.

All the quiet ones will get a daily thump,
And land on their bottoms with a heavy bump.
I'll twist their arms, cuss their mums, and swear,
Step on their toes, throw their bags in the air.

Don't you believe me? I'm not lying.
I won't stop till the whole school's crying.
I'll be the biggest bully of them all.
I'll be the total ruler of the school.

Because if everyone there is petrified
They'll never discover the secret I hide.

Questions for 'Big School':

- ❖ Do you think it's a good plan? Why or why not?
- ❖ If it works, is it a good plan?
- ❖ Can you do bad things in a good plan?
- ❖ What do you think the bully's secret might be?
- ❖ Could the bully have any other plans instead? Would they be better?

It's the Rules!

Why should I be nice to people?
Why should I not lie?
Why should I be good at all
Or not steal things, why oh why?

It's the rules.

Who makes these silly rules anyway?
No one asked me about them
Shouldn't there be a vote or something,
One that includes everyone?

It's the rules.

I'm going to make a rule,
A rule to rule all rules
And it's this: from here on in
The rule will be:

NO RULES!

Questions for 'It's the Rules!':

- ❖ Should we have rules?

- ❖ Should we ever break rules?

- ❖ If the rule was 'No rules!', what would it be like?

- ❖ Is it possible to have such a rule?

- ❖ Why do we have rules?

- ❖ If you lived on an island by yourself, like Robinson Crusoe, would you need rules to live by?

- ❖ Where do the rules come from?

Are You Free?

Bite

I really like chips
With ketchup on
But from this moment on
I don't!

I used to hate vegetables
Or anything green,
But not any more
I won't.

Chips are *disgusting*
Greens are *divine*
I've told my tongue
The new rules.

But what's going to happen
The next time I sit
Down at the table
And drool?

Will my tongue obey?
Do as it's told?
Like what I told it
To like?

Can I want
What I want
Whenever I want?

Or will my tongue
Turn out
To bite?

Questions for 'Bite':

❖ Can you want what you want whenever you want?

❖ Can you choose what you like?

❖ Can you choose what you want?

❖ What does the poem mean when it says 'Or will my tongue turn out to bite'?

❖ If you smoke a cigarette, is it a free choice?

❖ If you are a smoker and you smoke a cigarette, is it a free choice?

❖ If you are addicted to smoking but you want to give up, is that a free choice?

❖ What is a choice?

Déjà Vu

I watched a film today
And the characters didn't know
It was a film they were in.

But I knew there was nothing
They could do or say to change
What was happening.

I had seen it before.

Could *we* be the stars in our own film
Thinking we choose what we do
As the plot-line unfolds?

Could someone be watching our performance,
Becoming happy and sad,
As the story's retold?

Could *they* have seen it before?

Questions for 'Déjà Vu':

- ❖ What do you think the poem means?
- ❖ Could we be in a film? What might the poet mean by this idea?
- ❖ Is life like a film in any way?
- ❖ Are we in control of what happens to us?
- ❖ Is our future fixed or do we decide it?
- ❖ What about the characters in a film?
- ❖ What is déjà vu?

Asteroid

A mighty hunk of granite
Begins its slavish flight
Traversing distance infinite
Without meaning, without sight

Its destination written
Its target always there,
Just waiting for it, sitting
In an endless, sightless stare

When granite and Earth meet
After inexorable toil
It seems a plan-less feat
But for the thread that linked their soil.

Questions for 'Asteroid':

- ❖ If you kick a ball, is where it ends up determined by how it's kicked?

- ❖ There is an old Chinese saying, 'Endings are contained in their beginnings'. Once something begins does that mean that the end is inevitable?

- ❖ Is what you do at the end of your life determined by what happens at the beginning of your life?

- ❖ If so, does that mean that everything is planned?

- ❖ Are some things determined and other things not?

- ❖ Do things happen with or without meaning and purpose?

- ❖ Does how the universe begins determine everything that happens in the universe?

- ❖ If so, would that include you and me?

- ❖ Is what is going to happen determined?

Lines

I follow these lines
I find in the road
I weave in between them
I go where they go.

But way up ahead
The lines have all gone
Leaving me
By myself to press on.

Where do I go
With no lines to decide,
With nothing to guide me
And nowhere to hide?

The road seems lonely
And lightless to tread.
Should I turn back
Or continue ahead?

Shall I decide
For myself, win or lose?
Please tell me:
Is that what you think I should choose?

Questions for 'Lines':

- ❖ What do you think the poet is doing in the poem?
- ❖ What do you think the poem means?
- ❖ What is the poet trying to choose?
- ❖ Why does the poet ask the question at the end?
- ❖ Should we make our own choices in life?
- ❖ When should we listen to others?
- ❖ Is it better to choose for ourselves or to let others choose for us?
- ❖ Do you have to choose whether to choose or not?
- ❖ The philosopher Jean-Paul Sartre said we are 'condemned to be free'. What did he mean? And do you agree?
- ❖ What is a choice?
- ❖ Are we really free to choose?

It Wasn't Me!

When I ate the chocolate cake
There was nothing I could do, sir,
It wasn't me that made me eat it
It was my tongue and taste buds thereupon, sir,
I tried to resist, tried to look away
But the cake kept calling to me, sir,
I'm disposed to be weak around chocolate cake
It's the way I'm made, it's my family-make
And if it's down to me it's totally hopeless
I'm just a poor, innocent victim of deliciousness,
you see, sir!

Questions for 'It Wasn't Me!':

❖ Is the speaker in the above poem responsible for eating the cake?

❖ Is he/she right to blame their taste buds?

❖ Can you blame your parents for your weaknesses? Your genes perhaps?

❖ Are you free to resist temptations? If you fail can you blame anyone or anything?

❖ When are you not responsible for doing something?

Outroduction

Bliss

Blue is blue
What's true is true
Two and two
Is four!

It's really very
preliminary
I want to hear
No more

Silly talking
Billy *squawking,*
I've had enough
Of this

Philosophy,
So leave me be
In ignoramus'
Bliss!

Questions for 'Bliss':

- ❖ What is the poet trying to express?

- ❖ Do you agree with what the poet is expressing?

- ❖ What is the point of philosophy?

- ❖ Is it better to be a satisfied pig or a dissatisfied human?

- ❖ The philosopher Socrates famously said, 'The unexamined life is not worth living.' What do you think he meant by this? Do you agree with him or not?

- ❖ Is it better to be in ignorant bliss or is it better to know the truth, however uncomfortable or unpleasant it may be?

Appendix I: How To Use a Thoughting

Running an enquiry with a group of children

1. Choose a Thoughting that you like, but one where you are not sure what the 'answers' actually are (otherwise you might lead the children to them).

2. Begin by reading the poem out loud. Many of them are meant to have a comical effect, so use voices or pauses – anything to breathe life into it. Apart from perhaps one or two, they are not meant to be read solemnly.

3. When you finish, give the children about one minute to think about the poem in silence. Try asking them to remember as much of it as they can in their head.

4. Read the poem again. If it is a difficult or long poem then project the poem using an interactive whiteboard whilst you read it. You may decide to read it once without projection and then project it for the second reading.

5. Once you have read the poem for a second time, and if it is appropriate, hand out a paper copy of the poem

to the pairs or groups. Either way, from now on the children should be able to see the poem.

6. Give the children about two minutes to talk in pairs or small groups about the poem. Make sure the task is open-ended at this stage. You could give them the following questions: (1) What did they think of the poem? and/or (2) What do they think it means?

7. Stop them and explain that the next task is to think of a question about the poem that they would like to discuss with the class (one question for each pair or group).

8. Go around the class whilst they are talking in their groups and find out as many of the questions they have formulated as possible. Write any interesting ones down (from whatever point of view you are approaching this exercise, e.g. literacy, science, philosophy).

9. Choose an order for the interesting questions that have been generated (this allows you to prioritise the ones you think will be fruitful without rejecting others) or allow the children to vote from the list on which question they would like to explore first. (You could allow the discussion to go on for as long as you like or you may decide to set a time limit for each question's discussion, e.g. 10 or 15 minutes.)

10. Alternatively, you could use one of the questions printed below each poem. A good way to combine these approaches is to listen to the children when they are talking about the poem at the beginning to see if any of their ideas and discussions resembles the prepared questions. You could then use this criterion

to decide which one you choose, so that the decision comes from both the teacher and the children.

11. Then run a class discussion – or enquiry. If you don't already have your own way of doing a philosophical enquiry (or even if you do!) try The Philosophy Foundation's PhiE method (see *The If Machine* by Peter Worley (Continuum, 2010) and/or *The Philosophy Shop* edited by Peter Worley (Crown House, 2012) or Matthew Lipman's P4C 'Community of Enquiry' method (visit http://p4c. com).

Further ideas for your poetry-led enquiries

Especially if the poems rhyme, then, once you have read the poem once or twice, leave out the last word of each couplet and allow the children to finish it. This can help them, particularly the younger ones, engage with the poem more fully.

To aid their memory, use facial expressions, actions and/or hand movements. Encourage them to join in with the movements; then, later on, use the movement-cues to encourage the children to recite the poem. Use prompts only when needed, such as the first two words of a line or couplet.

You could also provide them with a copy of a poem but with certain words missing – especially the rhyming ones. Allow them to think of a word to go in the space. Later, you can compare what they have chosen with the author's original word(s). Ask them which they prefer and why.

Appendix II: Sample Lesson Plan[1]

This activity is based around 'Between My Ears' (see page 12) and is suitable for Year 3 and upwards. The aim of this lesson plan is to encourage the children to make a distinction between physical and non-physical properties of the mind and/or brain. This encourages them to 'discover' abstract nouns in the context of non-abstract entities such as 'the body'.

1. Read the poem to the class.

2. Give them some silent thinking time to take it in.

3. Read it again, but this time ask them if there are any words or phrases that they don't understand.

4. When you finish the second reading, take questions. Expect queries about words such as 'infinite' and 'width'. Rather than explain the words yourself, ask if anyone else in the class can explain the word or phrase. They may be able to do this because they know the word or, better still, they may be able to surmise its meaning (or approximate meaning) from the semantic context. To help them with this, recite the context to them and ask what they think it might

---

1 Many more lesson plans for *Thoughtings* will be available to members of The Philosophy Foundation website (www.philosophy-foundation.org). The site will also be regularly updated with new lesson plans.

mean. Make any clarifications or corrections before moving on.

5. Hand out copies of the poem to the class with the children in pairs, but print the poem large enough for the paper to be placed on the floor so that they can read it without having to hold the paper. This minimises distractions. Or project the poem on the interactive whiteboard.

6. You could ask the class what they think the poem is saying or what it means.

7. Task 1: Ask the children to say what they think is between their ears, but in order to encourage diversity of ideas towards non-physical properties set the following stipulation: everyone must contribute but there should be no repetition. This task begins easy but ends hard. Encourage children to help each other out towards the end. Note their suggestions on the board. You may expect the list to include physical words like 'brain', 'eyes', 'skull' and so on but you should look out for any non-physical words such as 'mind', 'knowledge' or 'thoughts' (all examples from Year 3).

8. Task 2: Distinguish between the two kinds of property (physical/non-physical) in some way, such as by using different colours or circling one kind of word. Ask the children if they can say what is different between the two sets of words (e.g. 'You can actually feel your skull, but ideas are invisible').

9. Task 3: Once they have identified the difference, ask them to continue adding to the 'non-physical' list, especially if this is much smaller than the 'physical' list (as you would expect it to be). Further suggestions

Appendix II: Sample Scheme of Work

from Year 3 classes have included 'ideas', 'the music I hear in my head,' information' and 'feelings'.

Extension activity

This extension activity was inspired by the child who said 'the music I hear in my head.'

1. Get the children to sing a well-known tune such as 'Happy Birthday', but silently in their heads. Conduct them and silently mouth the words making sure no one sings out loud.

2. Once they have finished, ask them whether they think they have just heard the song or not.

3. Ask the same question to your colleagues in the staffroom and your friends in the pub!

Questions

❖ What is sound?

❖ What is hearing?

❖ What is music?

❖ Can sound be imaginary?

❖ If a profoundly deaf person, such as the percussionist Evelyn Glennie, feels music through its vibration, are they 'hearing' the music?

Thoughtings

* Beethoven was deaf when he composed his famous
  'Ode to Joy' (Symphony No. 9). Did Beethoven ever
  hear his tune?

* When you hear music, where is the music? In the air?
  In your mind? In the instruments? Where?

For further extension activity ideas, see the list of questions
at the end of the poem 'Between My Ears'.

Other Thoughtings you could use as extensions to 'Between
My Ears' include:

* Ideas
* The Thought
* Infinity Add One
* Space